D0975392

A Gift For

From

Bear Hugs

Cheerful Thoughts, Poetry and
Scripture on Love and Friendship

GIFT BOOKS 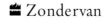 Zondervan

BOK5044

There's happiness in little things,
There's joy in passing pleasure.
But friendships are, from year to year,
The best of all life's treasure.

Your friendship means so much to me—
no one else can see me and my life as you
do. Your understanding and thoughtfulness
have helped me remember to be as patient
with others as you have always been with me.

A friend loves at all times.

PROVERBS 17:17

Rivers are like lives.
The more contributions they gain
from friendships, the bigger they
grow. Friendly, quiet little streams that
join them in their long journey to the
sea, make them strong and mighty.
The helpful contributions of love and
kindness we gain from friends make
our journey of life better and richer.

Where two or three come
together in my name,
there am I with them.

MATTHEW 18:20

A friend is someone to whom
you can talk forever and still
find things to say, but who
doesn't always need words to
know how you feel.

CONOVER SWOFFORD

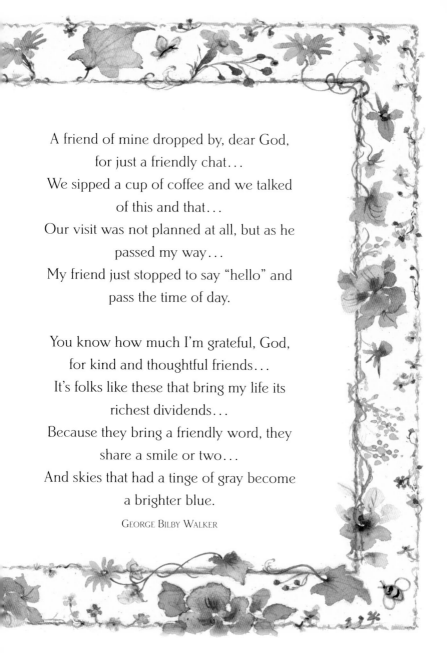

A friend of mine dropped by, dear God,
for just a friendly chat…
We sipped a cup of coffee and we talked
of this and that…
Our visit was not planned at all, but as he
passed my way…
My friend just stopped to say "hello" and
pass the time of day.

You know how much I'm grateful, God,
for kind and thoughtful friends…
It's folks like these that bring my life its
richest dividends…
Because they bring a friendly word, they
share a smile or two…
And skies that had a tinge of gray become
a brighter blue.

GEORGE BILBY WALKER

A real friend is one who will
continue to talk to you over
the back fence even though he knows
he's missing his favorite
television program.

Kind words, warm hearts and trust
that's earned is friendship's start.

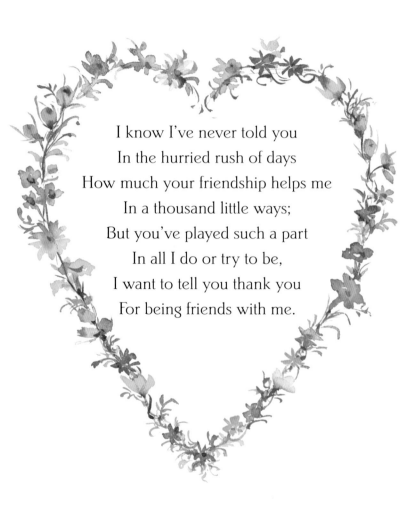

I know I've never told you
In the hurried rush of days
How much your friendship helps me
In a thousand little ways;
But you've played such a part
In all I do or try to be,
I want to tell you thank you
For being friends with me.

Oh, the comfort, the inexpressible comfort of feeling safe with a person; having neither to weigh thoughts nor measure words, but to pour them all out, just as they are, chaff and grain together, knowing that a faithful hand will take and sift them, keep what is worth keeping and then, with the breath of kindness, blow the rest away.

GEORGE ELIOT

Be completely humble and gentle;
be patient, bearing with one
another in love.

EPHESIANS 4:2

A real friend believes in the
real you, even when
you doubt yourself.

Some people have their first dollar. The
person who is really rich is the one who
still has his first friend.

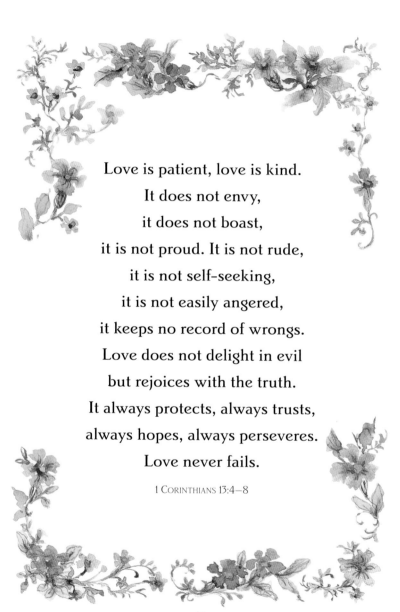

Love is patient, love is kind.
It does not envy,
it does not boast,
it is not proud. It is not rude,
it is not self-seeking,
it is not easily angered,
it keeps no record of wrongs.
Love does not delight in evil
but rejoices with the truth.
It always protects, always trusts,
always hopes, always perseveres.
Love never fails.

1 CORINTHIANS 13:4–8

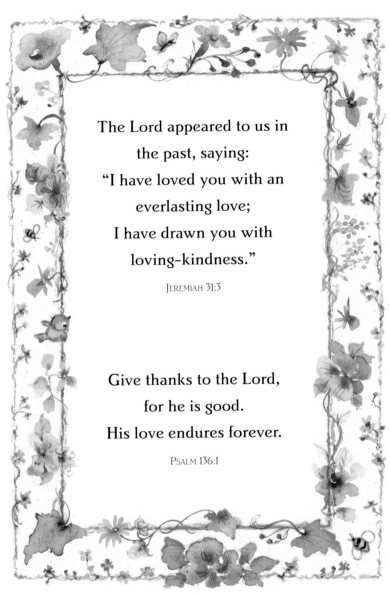

The Lord appeared to us in
the past, saying:
"I have loved you with an
everlasting love;
I have drawn you with
loving-kindness."

JEREMIAH 31:3

Give thanks to the Lord,
for he is good.
His love endures forever.

PSALM 136:1

Love is a gift sent from on high
To unite souls as one
And make sorrow fly.
Hold dear as a diamond
The gift from above;
To make life worth living
Just follow God's love.

The warming hearth of friendship
is built just one brick at a time.

Friendship is a chain of gold
Shaped in God's all perfect mold.
Each link a smile, a laugh, a tear,
A grip of the hand, a word of cheer.
Steadfast as the ages roll,
Binding closer soul to soul.
No matter how far or heavy the load,
Sweet is the journey on friendship's road.

A friend stands by
When storm clouds fly.
She's there through
thick and thin.
And when you really
need some help
She even steps right in.

Two are better than one,
because they have a good
return for their work:
If one falls down,
his friend can help him up.
But pity the man who falls
and has no one to help him up!

ECCLESIASTES 4:9–10

A true friend warms you with her presence, trusts you with her secrets and remembers you in her prayers.

**I thank my God every time
I remember you. In all my prayers
for all of you, I always pray with joy.**

PHILIPPIANS 1:3–4

The joy of being friends is just
A simple code of faith and trust,
A homey comradeship that stays
The threatened fear of darker days;
The kind of faith that brings to light
The good, the beautiful, and bright;
And best and blest, and true and rare—
Is having friends who love and care!

In our friendship, God seems to
weave together all the unique
threads of our personalities—
bright, quiet, coarse or fine—until
we find we have been stitched
into that beautiful coat of many
colors and textures called love.

A friend is a present
which you give yourself.

ROBERT LOUIS STEVENSON

May your joys be deep as the ocean,
Your sorrows as light as its foam.

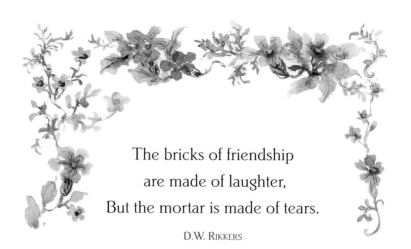

The bricks of friendship
are made of laughter,
But the mortar is made of tears.

D.W. RIKKERS

There is a time for everything,
and a season for every
activity under heaven:
a time to weep and
a time to laugh,
a time to mourn and
a time to dance.

ECCLESIASTES 3:1, 4

May you find friends
wherever you go,
And happily live while here below.
May you prove faithful,
kind, and true
To all your friends and
they to you.

MINNIE SIDDERS

A real friend loves you as you are—
and as you dream to become.

We can do no great things—
only small things with great love.

MOTHER TERESA

We love because he first loved us.
He has given us this command:
Whoever loves God must also love his brother.

1 JOHN 4:19, 21

Remember friends when far away;
Embrace those who are near.
Cherish those who are your friends,
Forever and sincere.

If the while I think on thee, dear friend,
All losses are restored and sorrows end.

WILLIAM SHAKESPEARE

"Don't urge me to leave you or to turn
back from you. Where you go I will go,
and where you stay I will stay. Your people
will be my people
and your God my God."

RUTH 1:16

A friend is one
in front of whom
you can be
your own true self.

God who is love…simply cannot help
but shed blessing upon blessing upon us.
We do not need to beg,
for he simply cannot help it!

Hannah Whitall Smith

**We know and rely on the love God has
for us. God is love. Whoever lives in
love lives in God, and God in him.**

1 John 4:16

Upon your heart like paper white,
Let none but friends presume to write;
And may each line with friendship given
Direct the senders' thoughts to Heaven.

Follow the way of love.

1 CORINTHIANS 14:1

It's only with the heart that one can see clearly.
The most important things are invisible to the eyes.

ANTOINE DE SAINT-EXUPERY

A real friend makes a difference
in your life, without choosing
your path for you.

He who loves a pure heart
and whose speech is gracious
will have the king for his friend.

PROVERBS 22:11

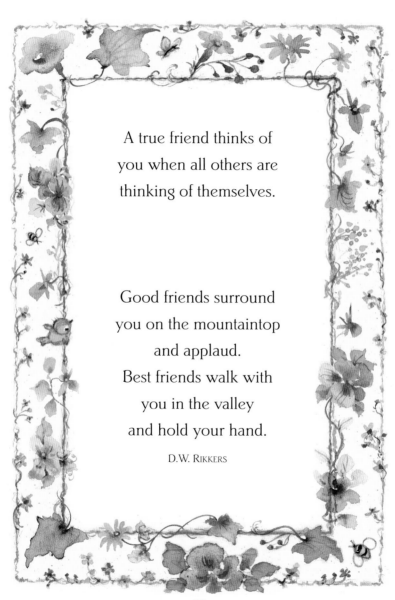

A true friend thinks of
you when all others are
thinking of themselves.

Good friends surround
you on the mountaintop
and applaud.
Best friends walk with
you in the valley
and hold your hand.

D.W. RIKKERS

Some take their gold
in minted mold
And some in harps hereafter;
But give me mine
in friendship fine;
Keep the change in laughter.

How great is the love
the Father has lavished on us,
that we should be called
children of God!

1 JOHN 3:1

Let love and faithfulness never leave you;
bind them around your neck, write them
on the tablet of your heart.

PROVERBS 3:3

We are not friends for fashion's sake;
We are not friends for fame,
But so that we remembered be
When someone speaks our name.

God is love.

1 JOHN 4:8

Dear friend, I pray...
that all may go well with you.

3 JOHN 2

A real friend invites you to come in
even when the house is messy.

The ornaments of a house
are the friends who visit it.

"Stay" is a charming word
in a friend's vocabulary.

Louisa May Alcott

There's a special kind of freedom
friends enjoy. Freedom to share
innermost thoughts, to show
their true feelings. The freedom
to simply be themselves.

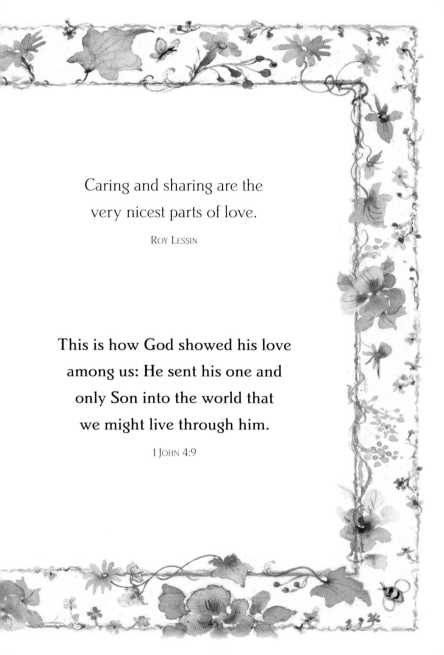

Caring and sharing are the
very nicest parts of love.

ROY LESSIN

This is how God showed his love
among us: He sent his one and
only Son into the world that
we might live through him.

1 JOHN 4:9

Jesus is a friend with whom you can feel safe.

JONI EARECKSON TADA

God has said, "Never will I leave you; never
will I forsake you." So we say with confidence.
"The Lord is my helper; I will not be afraid."

HEBREWS 13:5, 6

Bear with each other and forgive whatever grievances you may have against one another. Forgive as the Lord forgave you. And over all these virtues put on love, which binds them all together in perfect unity.

COLOSSIANS 3:13–14

Friends and family are a treasure from this life
that we may keep in the next.

Dear friends, let us love one another, for love comes from God.

1 JOHN 4:7

God's healing love will reach right down and make you whole again.

JONI EARECKSON TADA

The hands of God will hold us close in ways that no earthly friend ever could. You have a Father…Lover…Friend… and Home in heaven. God is as near as you'll allow him to be.

MARY PIELENZ HAMPTON

Friendships that have stood the test—
Time and change—are surely best;
Brow may wrinkle, hair grow gray,
Friendship never knows decay.

JOSEPH PARRY

Friendships are the heart's
great treasure,
Pearls of price no scale
can measure.
Promise of silver, gift of gold
Found in friends
both new and old.

A real friend loves
you for who you are
but tells you the truth
when you need to hear it.

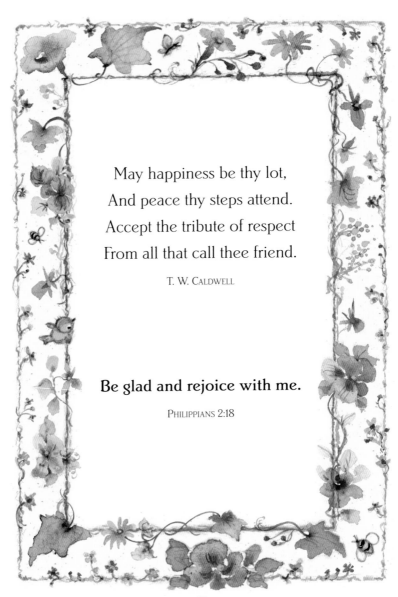

May happiness be thy lot,
And peace thy steps attend.
Accept the tribute of respect
From all that call thee friend.

T. W. CALDWELL

Be glad and rejoice with me.

PHILIPPIANS 2:18

Jesus said, "Love each other as I have
loved you. Greater love has no one
than this, that he lay down his life for
his friends. You are my friends if you do
what I command. I have called you
friends, for everything that
I learned from my Father I have
made known to you."

JOHN 15:12–15

God loves each of us as if
there were only one of us.

SAINT AUGUSTINE

Into any ordinary day,
the grace of friendship
may break through
with unexpected gifts
as bright as any rainbow.

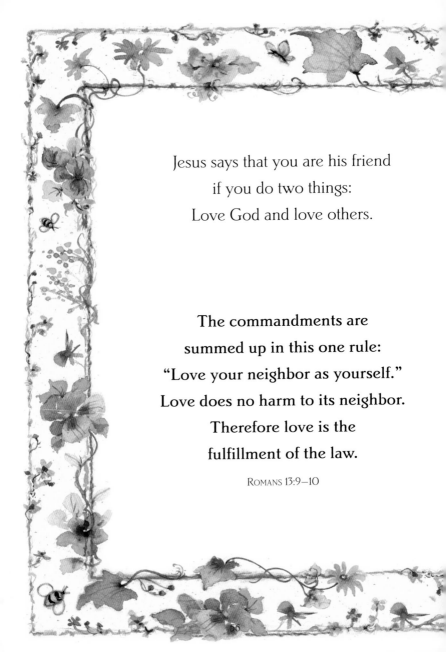

Jesus says that you are his friend
if you do two things:
Love God and love others.

The commandments are
summed up in this one rule:
"Love your neighbor as yourself."
Love does no harm to its neighbor.
Therefore love is the
fulfillment of the law.

ROMANS 13:9–10

Friendship is a living thing
that lasts only as long
as it is nourished with
kindness and understanding.

The love of God is not mere sentimentality;
it is the most practical thing for
the saint to love as God loves.
The springs of love are in God, not in us.

OSWALD CHAMBERS

Life has no blessing like a prudent friend.

A true friend doesn't sympathize
with your weakness;
instead he helps summon your strength.

Do everything in love.

1 CORINTHIANS 16:14

The finest kind of friendship is
between people who expect a
great deal of each other but
never ask it.

SYLVIA BREMER

A real friend forgives your mistakes
and doesn't remember to be offended.

Love each other deeply,
because love covers over
a multitude of sins.

1 PETER 4:8

There's a comforting thought
at the close of the day,
When I'm weary and lonely and sad,
That sort of grips hold of my crusty old heart
And bids it be merry and glad.
It gets in my soul and drives out the blues,
And finally thrills through and through.
It is just a sweet memory that chants the refrain:
"I'm glad for good friends just like you!"

When the golden sun is sinking,
And God's sweet night begins to fall,
When of absent friends you're thinking
Breathe a prayer for one and all.